Copyright © Aditi Nag
All Rights Reserved.

Made with ❤ on the BookLeaf Publishing Platform
www.bookleafpub.in
www.bookleafpub.com

The Lost Dairy

A soul on a journey, uncovering the
illusions of this world.

Aditi Nag

Dedication

To my beloved parents—
Your unwavering love and silent strength have carried
me through every high and held me through every low.
You are my first home, my deepest faith, and my
constant light.

To my husband—
Your belief in me has been the wind beneath every leap.
With your love, patience, and partnership, the impossible
feels possible, and the journey feels like home. Thank
you for standing beside me with dignity, grace, and
boundless support.

To my friends and well-wishers— You never let me give
up. You saw the fire in me before I did. Thank you for
pushing me to dream bigger, do more, and believe that
one day—I will. And to you, my dear reader— This book
is for the relentless, the dreamers, the doers—those who
never settle for what's handed to them. Keep striving.
Keep believing.
Your day may not
be tomorrow, but one day—it will be all yours.

Preface

The Lost Diary is more than just a book—it is a journey through the untold stories of the heart, captured in the silent pages where words once lingered, waiting to be heard. It is a revelation of the truths and lies that often hide behind the smiles we wear, exposing the raw realities that shape our lives. This book is dedicated to those who seek to connect with the soul's deepest emotions—those who have questioned the world around them and yearn to uncover the illusions that bind us. It is for the ones who, like me, are on a quest to explore the hidden truths, to seek answers in a world that often leaves more questions than solutions. The Lost Diary is created with love, built from a tapestry of emotions that span across relationships, struggles, and triumphs. It speaks to the universal experiences we all share— whether the support of family, the bond of friendship, the ache of loss, or the unwavering faith that drives us forward. It is a reflection on the strength to prove oneself, to overcome, and to remain steadfast in the pursuit of becoming the purest version of ourselves. This book is for those who have faced adversity and have still chosen to rise, for those who believe that no matter the obstacles, the light within can still shine. It is a testament to the power of faith, love, and the relentless desire to find meaning in the midst of chaos. As you turn these pages, I invite you to walk with me through the moments of vulnerability and strength, to uncover the truths that may resonate with your own journey. May you find a part of yourself in these words, and may they inspire you to continue your own quest for truth, love, and self-discovery.

Acknowledgements

I am deeply grateful for the opportunity to put my words, my emotions, and my journey into the form of this book. The creation of The Lost Diary has been a deeply personal endeavor, and I could not have reached this point without the unwavering support and encouragement of several remarkable individuals. First and foremost, I owe my deepest gratitude to my parents, whose love, guidance, and strength have been the foundation of everything I am.

Their belief in me has been a constant source of inspiration and motivation, helping me navigate every challenge along the way.

To my wonderful husband, thank you for being my rock, my partner, and my greatest supporter. Your faith in me, especially during the times when I doubted myself, has been invaluable. You have made this journey not just possible, but truly meaningful. Your love and belief have carried me further than I ever thought possible.

I would also like to extend my heartfelt thanks to the team at BookLeaf for providing me with the perfect platform to express my feelings and thoughts. Your dedication and professionalism have turned my dream into a reality. I am truly grateful for your support and for

helping me give my words a tangible form that will
hopefully resonate with many.
Lastly, I dedicate this book to all writers, especially
those who, like me, may have doubted whether their
voices could be
heard. If my story and my words can encourage
even one person to begin their own journey of
expression, then this endeavor will have been worth
every
moment.
Thank you all for believing in me and helping me
bring The Lost Diary to life.

1. Noise

I woke up one day to some noise,
Chanting things in a loud, crude voice.
Twisting my truth with selfish intention,
Shouting my name just for attention.

I love to care, I give my all,
But not everyone can take the fall.
I try and try to dodge the void,
Yet still, they choose to make some noise.

Not all are the same—I'll admit,
But some still try to make my heart split.
I won't stay quiet every day,
Don't cry when I've got truth to say.

I woke up one day to some noise,
They called me dumb, like I had no choice.
But I rise beyond their heavy bars,
Raising my voice, reaching for stars.
Seeking a space where silence brings peace,

Where the noise fades—and my soul finds release.

2. Distraction

Distraction—

a name,

a place,

a fleeting thing.

Still, I wonder why they called me king.

It's not a throne—just a broken seat

in a game where hearts are used for defeat.

People play like life's a test,

treating souls like less,

while pretending it's all in jest.

I don't know why they see me as waste—

like something thrown out

in a world of haste.

It's not the place that drags you back—

it's the people,

the looks,

the subtle attack.

You thought they were kind,

soft to the touch—
but kindness was never really that much.

It's not about girl or boy—
a soul is a soul,
and even joy
must struggle daily just to breathe,
just to wake,
just to believe.

Distraction doesn't conquer all—
some of us rise,
some stand tall.
Focus is rare, but it's a shield—
the one thing fake hands cannot wield.

This world—
a board of snakes and ladders,
of liars and silent soul shatterers.
Some offer ladders, some wear a smile,
but lead you down
with poison the whole while.

Distraction creeps,
whispers your name,
makes you forget
why you entered the game.

It dims the dream,
it clouds the light,
pulls you from vision
into the night.

And in the end,
you're left to face
a quiet room,
an empty space—
where questions echo,

soft and grave:
*What did you lose
when you tried to be brave?*

3. The "T" of My Life

The "T" of my life stands for *Test*,
Which life throws at me till I rest.
The "T" stands for *Tears*,
That fall in joy or pain, through the years.

The "T" stands for *Transformation*,
Where I strive and push for elevation.
The "T" stands for *Trauma*,
Given by those who leave me in dilemma.

The "T" stands for the *Truth*,
The hidden facts that hit me in youth.
The "T" stands for *Terrific*,
Shaped by my will, strong and prolific.

The "T" stands for *Toxic*,
From people whose drama feels caustic.
The "T" stands for *Thankful*,
For those who stood by when life felt painful.

4. A Friend Like This

I met a soul, so sweet, so bright, A gentle face, a heart of
light.
He sat behind, a quiet grace, In that old classroom,
shared space.
Strangers then— but fate had plans, Awkward words
turned into hands reaching out through laughs and days,
and friendship bloomed in simple ways.

Months turned into rolling years,
Filled with joy, and silly cheers.
But time, as ever, made its call— We walked new roads,
beyond school walls.
College came with distant dreams,
Different paths and separate scenes.
New cities held our hopes and fears,
Yet still we spoke across the years-

Through emails, chats, and midnight snaps,
We shared our wins, our little gaps.

New foods, new friends, late study nights, Mixed with
stress and future flights.
But slowly, life began to race, No pause, no breath, no
gentle space.
Happiness grew hard to find, Buried in the daily grind.
Then came a storm— and with it, a ring,
A voice from past that made heart sing.

"It's me," he said, "your friend from school,
I'm off abroad—it feels so cool!"
My heart leapt high in silent glee, Yet mourned the space
he'd take from me.
I wished him well, my voice sincere,
Still holding back a quiet tear.
And months later, I found my way
A job won through a thousand days
Of passion, sweat, and sleepless nights,
I called to share my earned delight.
But fate again had something planned—
A stranger's voice, not one I'd manned.
"This is the hospital," they said.

My heart turned cold. My soul felt dread.
An accident.
He's in a fight.
Could I come?
Could I catch a flight?

I didn't think. I didn't wait.
I packed my hope, embraced his fate.
And flew across both sky and fear
To be the one to stand right near. And there he was—my
friend, my
light,

In pain, but glowing, weak yet bright.
"How did you come? How did you know?"
His voice was soft, his words were low.
I answered not with lips, but eyes
A promise kept. A bond that ties. We hugged like time
had slipped away,
And let our tears find words to
say.

In grief and joy, in ache and bliss
We felt what truly friendship is. Because a friend who
stands this close,
Through storm and change, through highs and lows, Is
rare as stars on moonless nights—
A glowing thread, a sacred light. A friend like this— is
everything.

5. Why Me?

I watch the world go spinning
'round,
While I toil, unseen, unheard, From dusk till dawn, a
silent sound—
My voice drowned out, my dreams deferred.

They win the praise, the gilded prize,
For plans I dreamt through sleepless nights.
A smile I wear, but deep inside, A bittersweet and silent
fight.
I give my care, I give my all, Yet love pours into
stranger's hands.

And mine? A pot cracked, or too small
To hold the weight of hopeful plans.
I see the doors swing open wide
For others. Mine remain untouched.

In corners where lost wishes hide,

I wait for years that ask too much.
Each night, alone, I lie and ache,
As heart and hope begin to fray.

"Why always me?"—a silent quake
That shakes my soul, then fades away.
A loop that spins within my mind, No start, no end, no
peace to find.

6. Guardians

I believe in dreams— In heroes, too—
Not those who soar across the skies,
But those who walk with wornout shoes,
With tired hands and gentle eyes.

I see my parents, brave and still, Warding off the world's
sharp edge,
Holding storms with quiet will— My sacred shield, my
living pledge.
I glimpse a stranger's selfless
grace,

Offering bread, a smile, a space. No wings adorn their
weathered skin,
Yet still, they lift the world within.
My teacher speaks in softer tones,
Yet moves the earth beneath my feet.
Through sleepless nights, through aching bones,
She builds a path where dreams can meet.

Her lessons etched in care and flame—
To teach me love, not just a name.
A soldier at the border stands, A friend who holds my
shaking hands,
A passerby who sees my fall, And stops—no question
asked at all.

They are the ones the stories miss,
The ones who guide with wordless bliss.
Guardians not of myth or lore, But of the love we're
searching for.

So be a light where shadows grow,
A flame for hearts too dim to show.
Give more than what you think
you own—
You'll find in that, you're not alone.

7. Scars

People drift like autumn leaves,
Coming, going—on their breeze.
They change with time, with whim, with tide,
Leaving marks they never tried

To see, to feel, or understand—
Scars etched by careless passing hands.
Scars—silent whispers on the skin,
Or buried deep where thoughts begin.

They bloom in places eyes can't trace,
On hearts, on hopes, on time and face.
Not all are beautiful, yet still,
They shape the soul, they bend the will.

Beauty fades like fleeting light,
But scars remain through endless night.
A tale they tell in broken lines—
Of battles fought, of twisted signs.

A map of pain, a truth laid bare,
A legacy that few will wear.
And in those scars, a truth remains:
The loss, the love, the silent chains.

They hold the echoes of "what if,"
Of paths not taken, hearts adrift.
A moment passed, a second missed—
A life that leaned toward the abyss.
Yet in those depths, a light can gleam—
A second chance, a distant dream.

To touch the pain without regret,
To feel what time won't let forget.
Not every wound becomes a wall
Some cracks can let the light in, after all.
Scars are cruel, but also kind—
They hurt, they heal, they free the mind.

And though unseen by naked eyes,
They speak in ways no mirror tries.
So wear them not with shame or fear—
But as the proof that you were here.

For every scar, both seen and veiled,
Tells of a heart that hoped, and failed—
Yet dared to love, to lose, to grow...
And that alone is beautiful.

8. Nevermind

A pure soul, aglow with light,
Untouched by the weight of practical plight.
Chasing dreams through endless skies,
For joy, for peace, for gentler highs.

A mind that blooms as seasons do—
Not time, but people, shape the view.
They teach us where our worth must lie,
To guard our pride, to dignify.
Then one day, fate softly plays,
You meet a soul who lights your days.

A beauty rare, both kind and wise
You see forever in their eyes.
You dream of life, of love, of grace,
Of quiet mornings face to face.
But destiny, with silent might,
Shifts the stars and dims the light.

You pass again, like strangers near,

No echoes left, no words to hear.
A handshake cold, a nod, a smile
As if you never shared a mile.

Unspoken truths begin to fade,
While questions linger, halfconveyed.
The heart still stirs, but can't rewind—
And so you breathe, and say: Nevermind.

9. The Lifeline

Life begins not with a cry, but a race⁻
Of name, of fame, of time, of place.
A journey drawn in silent grace,
Etched by God on each hand's face.
These lines—unseen scripts we bear,
Whispers of fate written with care.

They curve and cross with paths unknown,
Yet still, we walk, our will alone.
Time shifts like sand beneath our feet,
The lines may blur, the world repeat.
But ask yourself what holds more weight:
The fate you're told, or the hands you create?

Yes, luck and life play sacred parts,
But luck won't spark a lifeless heart.
When breath runs out and time won't bend,
No charm can bring it back again.
Still, these lines—they speak in code,

Of stories lived, of truths untold.

Some run straight, some twist and hide,
Yet all lead to the end we ride.
There's much to learn, to read, to feel,
In every crease, a truth revealed.
And sometimes, one soul's lines align,
Walking beside you—hand in hand with time.

Life is chaos, joy, and pain,
A storm, a song, a passing train.
It marches on through love and hate,
Toward the stillness we all await.
So here's to lifelines—raw and real,
Uneven, wild, yet they reveal.

That what makes sense may come too late,
But still, each line participates
In shaping who we are, and why...
Until we reach our final sigh.

10. Mind-games

Players aren't made—they're born from flame,
Drawn to the thrill, the rush of the game.
Not of dice or cards or fate alone,
But of minds, where darker seeds are sown.

Some play with time, with trust, with name,
But the sharpest play the subtle game—
Of bending thoughts and planting doubt,
Until the heart is inside out.

He wears a coat, he holds your hand,
She smiles as if she understands.
Yet behind the mask, a twist, a spin—
They play to lose, and still they win.

At school, at work, or in the nest,
Where love should bloom and souls should rest,
They twist the truth, rewrite your page,
And call it life—it's just a stage.

The saddest twist: you play along,
You question right, you silence wrong.
Their whispers shape your inner voice,
Till you're the villain by your choice.

They never stole your world outright,
They made you hand it, piece by piece, in fright.
With every rule you let them make,
They watch you bend, they watch you break.

But rise—reclaim your rightful part,
Take back your mind, protect your heart.
They fear the truth you truly are,
A blazing soul, a rising star.

So play their game, if you must, with care—
Reverse the rules, strip masks laid bare.
And while they bluff with poisoned hands,
You'll stand with strength they'll never understand.

Stop the mindgames. Break the chain.
Let courage course through every vein.
For those who play with hearts in shame—
Will one day burn by their own game.

11. Success

What is success, if not a dream in disguise?
A whisper of hope beneath tired eyes.
Is it a goal, a name, a fleeting spark—
Or just the light we chase in dark?

A question with no perfect key,
An answer shaped unpredictably.
A common quest with rare reward,
A silent war not often scored.

It sounds like a noun—a person, a place,
A title worn like silk or lace.
But deeper still, it's something
more—

A lesson carved in life's great lore.
Belonging to humankind, it speaks Of kindness wrapped
in restless weeks.
It cannot be weighed or boxed in lines,
For success, like stars, forever shines.

It comes with hope, it leaves with grace,
It shifts with time, it changes face.

It grows in thoughts, in how we strive,
In what we give to keep dreams alive.
An evolution born of sweat and soul,
Of breaking down to reach a whole.

By the people, of the people—yes,
It's found in failure and progress.
We run this race with trembling hands,
On shifting roads and sinking sands.
Yet we decide, with heart sincere,
When to push the gear—or steer.

For sometimes, life will throw you pain,
Stone-shaped trials that feel like strain.
But polish them with grit and flame—
And they just might shine with diamond names.

12. Logic vs Emotion

It was a rain-washed day,
Clouds wept like memories unspoken.
A call pierced through the gray—
My friend, asking to share a token Of time, just one day.
Joy bloomed like sudden sun,
I danced through the silence,
Fixing lights that once flickered,
Chasing sounds that had fallen dumb.
She arrived, arms cradling a world—
Bags brimming with things she'd won.

Her laughter burst like wildfire,
Childlike wonder spilled as one.
She showed me treasures, new and bright,
Tales of purchases told in light—
Each trinket, each thread,
A silent scream: "Look what I've done instead!"
I smiled, caught in tangled delight,
But shadows whispered: "Is this joy, or spite?"
Then quiet.

She paused—
Realizing this stage was hers alone.
"Let's see," she murmured, "if there's something for you..."
And suddenly, I was unknown.
The room grew still,
Wine shimmered in crystal like held breath,
Starters untouched on a table of
While she searched for meaning,
A gift, or perhaps
Just time—
But neither came in form nor line.

Did she come bearing presents or presence?
Did she mean to share or to shine?
The moment teetered like a seesaw,
Between the heart and the spine.

She chose logic—clean and dry—
To measure joy by weight and buy.
I stood with soul uncloaked,
Choosing emotion—raw and woke—
To live, not show,
To feel, not owe,
With wisdom etched in quiet grace,
While hers was just
A pretty face

In a rainlit place.

13. The Knife Behind the Smile

I built my walls with words and trust,
Opened doors once sealed with rust.
Let in souls I thought were true,
Gave them light, gave them me— through and through.
They spoke in silk, with honeyed grace,
Wore masks of care upon their face.

I offered time, I gave my name,
Not knowing I'd be fuel for their game.
They took my kindness like it was owed,
Walked my heart like a beaten road.
Each promise made was laced with lies,
A dagger hidden in disguise.

They laughed in circles I couldn't hear,
My loyalty turned to souvenir.
"Look at the fool," they jest and grin,
"Trusted too deep, let the wrong one in."
They turned my silence into shame,

My truth became their drinking game.

I stood alone, a lesson learned,
While bridges burned and memories churned.
And yet I rise—not made of glass,
Not every scar means I won't surpass.
Their betrayal made a storm within,
But from that flood, I learned to swim.

So mock me, call me soft or blind,
But strength is forged in the kindest mind.
And those who play with others' grace,
Will one day beg for a saving face.

14. Across the Borderline

He wakes before the sun breaks sky,
A silent oath in every sigh.
Miles away from all he knows,
Where love once bloomed and stillness grows.
A boy, a friend, a lover true,
Wearing shoes worn thin by all he must do.

Not for glory, not for gain,
But for faces he sees when he closes the pain.
He serves the clock, he serves the land,
With blistered feet and calloused hands.
Each night, a letter he'll never send,
Words unsaid to love, to friend.

He keeps her voice in saved voicemails,
Their dreams replay in silent tales.
Plans sketched in the corners of Sleep:
A home, a trip, a promise to keep.
The border isn't just a line,

It's years and tears and borrowed time.

A distance wrapped in sacrifice,
Each step forward comes with a price.
He hides his ache behind routine,
Sips cold coffee, wipes thoughts clean.
But in his chest, a quiet war—
The need to give, the ache to soar.

Some nights, he whispers to the dark,
Of kisses missed, of walks in parks.
Of brothers laughing in the rain,
Of hands he'll hold again.
And when the time is right—he swears—
He'll cross with stories, not just stares.

He'll speak the words he never dared,
Not just feel them—he'll be prepared.
Until then, he'll endure the load,
On distant soil, a silent road.
A boy, a friend, a lover brave—
Who crossed the border not to escape, But to stay.

15. Truth or Dare

Is it truth, or is it dare?
Choosing one for life—what a fear.
Fear of losing someone near,
Yet brave enough to face what's clear.
People come and go with time,
With fleeting fame, and fading shine.

But those who stay—through storm and strife—
Are the quiet truths that shape your life.
Wanting the unwanted,
Revealing what's concealed—
That's the dare we often dodge,
But it's the pride of standing real.

A crowd surrounds, loud and wide,
But most have no spine to speak or decide.
Not all abuse is bruised and seen—
Some are technical,
Some political,
Lurking beneath a polished sheen.

Right or wrong?
It depends who cheers.
Supporters shape the narrative,
Whispering lies into willing ears.
Truth or dare—
it still breeds fear.
For people like me, It's clear:

I don't care who's standing behind,
Truth walks alone, But it's not blind.
For many, it's a twisted game,
They fear the truth, yet dare in vain.
Because they need a crowd to fight—
But truth stands quiet, And dare fakes light.

So choose your people carefully.
Your life will grow the way you bend it,
Shape it,
Feed it—truthfully or falsely.
Positive or negative,
It all grows with time—
Rooted in choices, phase by phase.

16. A Soulmate

A soul, an entity, a sacred flame,
A journey begun with a destined name.
One path, one mate, no fear of fate,
For with them, you're never late.
Just at the right place, at the right time,
Revealing truths through rhythm and rhyme.

Together, diving into horizons wide,
With love and wonder as your guide.
A soulmate, a lover, a lifelong friend,
A bond that time can never bend.
Someone to trust, with whom you share,
Each feeling, each wound, with tender care.

A soul of desire, of pure intention,
Holding hands through every dimension.
No storm, no hour can pull apart,
Two souls stitched with a single heart.
A light from heaven, sent from above,
To lead you to purpose, with endless love.

To bring joy, to breathe life into stone,
To see beyond what's ever been known.
A soulmate arrives like a magical spark,
Guiding your spirit out of the dark.
And even when time ceases to be
They remain, in love, for eternity.

17. The Treasure

Not all treasure gleams in gold,
Some shine in hearts we gently hold.
In quiet smiles, in whispered names,
In strangers turned to sacred flames.
A voice that says, "I see you still," When others scoff, or doubt your
doubt your
A hand that finds yours in the storm,
And builds a home where you feel warm.

This treasure lives in what we give,
In reasons not just to exist—but live.
A soul who loves the flawed and true,
Who walks the edge of dreams with you.

It's not a chest, it's not a throne,
But the feeling of not being alone.
Of someone who, without a script,
Knows your silence, every crypt.
It's every moment someone stays,
When life has turned a thousand ways.

It's every cheer when no one knew,
The fight you fought just to push through.

And sometimes treasure comes in tears,
In shared scars across the years.
When love is blind but always sees,
The art you give so selflessly.
Two hearts that meet, by chance, by fate,
Across the years, across the gate
Of loneliness and life's demands,
To hold each other with bare hands.
They don't just love what you become,
They love the places you came from.

Your cracks, your fire, your untold fight,
Your human soul in every light.
So here's to the treasures made of grace,
Of courage, love, and time and space.
A life secured not in control,
But in the warmth of one kind soul.

18. Adulthood

Once, I was cradled in warm arms,
Eyes wide to a world with no alarms.
Cried when it thundered, hid in fright,
But always knew I'd be alright.
Laughed for hours in muddy fields,
With scraped-up knees and dreams as shields.

Homework felt like the heaviest load,
Yet now I carry far greater roads.
Years slipped by like evening light,
And slowly, playtime turned to fight—

Not of fists, but of silent strain,
Of juggling joy with aching pain.
Now I walk through sleepless nights,
Chasing dawn with borrowed might.

No longer scared of the dark outside,
But of the silence I carry inside.
Friends, once close like summer air,

Are voices I now meet in prayer.

The games we played, the tales we spun—
All paused, all blurred, as the race begun.
My parents' backs have bowed with time,
Their steps are slower, their eyes still kind.
Now it's my turn to hold their hand,
To be their pillar, to help them stand.

A job, a dream, a family too—
Trying to hold what feels so few.
Balancing hopes like tightrope threads,
Where only one dream often treads.

Yes, adulthood is a silent vow—
To live not just for self, but how
We shape a world for those to come,
And honor where we've all come from.

And though the weight may break my sleep,
It's a promise I was born to keep.
From crying in the cradle's hood,
To building life—as I should.

19. All About You

You are the storm that makes no sound,
A whisper walking through a thundercloud.
Silent, but the fire in your chest— Speaks truths that
silence can't suppress.
You're gentle—

Yet carry steel beneath your skin. You smile at chaos,
But let no liar in.
You cry, not out of weakness, no
But when love in others dares to grow.
A sweet tear falls when someone shines,
Like you're proud, though no one's watching you this
time.

You laugh in rooms that drain your soul,
Not to join, but to feel whole.
Avoid the crowds, escape the glare,
Because you've learned: not all who hug you care.
You are the echo of quiet rage,
Turned soft with wisdom, aged by age.

You speak when silence just won't do—
And every word feels pure, feels true.
You're emotional, but not unwise,
You choose who sees behind your eyes.

Not everyone deserves the weight,
Of knowing why your shoulders break.
You evolve with every crashing tide,
Not losing self—just growing wide.
You're happy, yes—but sadness stays,
A quiet guest on brighter days.

And yet you give, and rise, and try,
Though often never knowing why.
The world takes pieces, leaves no sign—
And you ask softly, "What's the point, if none of this is
mine?"

But here's the truth you rarely see:
Your pain's not wasted, nor is "we.
You are the strength in every crack,
The soul that bends but still comes back.

20. Bloody Relation

I wore love like armor, Carved from my soul, not for
show.
Gave laughter in storms, stood tall when low,
Held hands that now throw stones in shadow.
I was the one—

The silent keeper of everyone's smile,
The fixer, the forgiver,
Running miles while they stood vile.
My heart beat louder for them than for me,
I bled trust like it was free.
And they?

They turned it into a weapon— glee.
Jealous eyes behind smiles I knew,
Whispers grew where roses once flew.
Not strangers—blood.

The ones who watched me rise... and schemed how to
undo.

They mocked my joy,
My wife—my pride, my light— Strong, radiant, by my side,
And our daughter, fierce flame in the night,
Who saw through their lies and chose what's right.

She taught me to see, to stand, to speak,
To find strength even when I felt weak.
"Let them play their dirty game," she said,
"Truth walks slow but strikes deep."

So now I wait—
Not in silence, but in storm.
My scars are not shame,
They're how comebacks are born.
This isn't just revenge—
It's reckoning wrapped in flame.

Every ounce of pain my mother swallowed,
Every silent scream my father followed—
Will rise in me, tenfold returned.
The tables are set. The lesson will be earned.

Let them smirk in their glassbuilt throne,
When it shatters, they'll stand alone.
For the one they betrayed,
Will return not broken—but remade.

I am coming back.
Not with hate, but with fire in my
eyes.

No more disguise.
Only truth that cuts, and time that tries.
They'll feel it—
The weight of all they did in vain.
Because I carry more than my name—
I carry a legacy forged in pain.

21. The Wandering Soul

I am the soul that walks unseen,
Across the veil where life has been.
Born in flesh, then freed in flame,
Each breath a whisper, each death the same.
From cradle's cry to funeral hymn,
I rise and fall at fate's own whim.

In every life, I stand once more—
Before two doors, one peace, one war.
Right and wrong, both call my name,
But only one can light the flame.

One path steeped in sacrifice,
The other cloaked in fleeting vice.
I've worn the crown, I've borne the chain,
Felt lover's kiss, and soldier's pain.
Each form a test, each breath a clue,
To find the truths I never knew.

I chase the peace I've never caught,

The sacred stillness sages sought.
In temples high or battle's roar,
I seek the key to something more.
A life to learn, to build, to break,
To give for love, not just to take.

And if I fail, the wheel returns,
In ash and tears, the lesson burns.
There is a death while still alive,
A silence deep where sorrows thrive.
A soul can ache within the skin,
While wearing smiles to hide what's in.

But if I rise from that despair,
Choose the light, lay ego bare,
Then karma bends, the stars align,
And heaven waits beyond the spine.
Not in clouds or gates of gold,
But in a heart that's brave and bold.

To do what's right, to walk with grace,
To leave a mark, not just a trace.
And if I fall, then let me fall
Learning still, beyond it all.
For I will rise, again, again—
A soul reborn through joy and pain.